song of solomon

the song of

solomon

authorised king james version

printed by authority

published by canongate

with an introduction by | a s byatt

First published in Great Britain in 1998
by Canongate Books Ltd
14 High Street, Edinburgh EH1 1TE

10 9 8 7 6 5 4 3 2

Introduction copyright © A S Byatt 1998
The moral right of the author has been asserted

British Library Cataloguing-in-Publication Data
A catalogue record is available on request from
the British Library

ISBN 0 86241 793 7

Typeset by Palimpsest Book Production
Book design by Paddy Cramsie
Printed and bound in Great Britain
by Caledonian International Book Manufacturing Ltd, Glasgow

a note about pocket canons

The Authorised King James Version of the Bible, translated between 1603–11, coincided with an extraordinary flowering of English literature. This version, more than any other, and possibly more than any other work in history, has had an influence in shaping the language we speak and write today. Presenting individual books from the Bible as separate volumes, as they were originally conceived, encourages the reader to approach them as literary works in their own right.

The first twelve books in this series encompass categories as diverse as history, fiction, philosophy, love poetry and law. Each Pocket Canon also has its own introduction, specially commissioned from an impressive range of writers, which provides a personal interpretation of the text and explores its contemporary relevance.

A S Byatt was born in Yorkshire. Her novels include Shadow of a Sun, The Game, The Virgin in the Garden *and* Still Life. *In 1990 her best-selling novel* Possession *won the Booker Prize and the Irish Times/Aer Lingus International Fiction Prize. Her other books include* Angels and Insects *and two short story collections,* The Matisse Stories *and* The Djinn in the Nightingale's Eye. *Her latest novel,* Babel Tower, *was published to great acclaim in 1996. As well as being a distinguished literary critic, she has served as a judge of various literary prizes, including the Booker. A S Byatt was appointed* CBE *in 1990 for her work as a writer. She lives in London.*

introduction by a s byatt

The Song of Songs is a cry of erotic longing and a description of erotic bliss. It is a lyrical drama whose speakers and episodes run into each other as in a dream or a vision. There is a female voice, which is both virginal and knowing, triumphant and lost. There is a male voice, impatient, exulting, wooing. There is a chorus of unseen commentators, and other groups, the women of Jerusalem, the watchmen, the threescore valiant men who stand around the bed of Solomon. The scene shifts from walled garden to walled city to green bedchamber to the mountains. The woman is black but comely; the man is white and ruddy, with a head like fine gold and with bushy locks, black as a raven. The ending is abrupt and the story is fragmentary. It is a canonical biblical text, and yet there is no mention of God or of religion. It haunts many cultures, eastern and western.

It was ascribed, along with *Ecclesiastes* and *Proverbs*, to King Solomon, son of David. Solomon, according to *The Book of Kings*, had 'seven hundred wives, princesses, and three hundred concubines'; he was famous both for his wisdom and his lechery. The *Song* was thought to refer to his marriage with the daughter of Pharoah, or to his fabled meeting with the Queen of Sheba, who tested him with riddles, the answers to which were to do with the bodies of women.* Jewish commentators saw the woman as Israel, black with her sins; the reading of the *Song* was prescribed during the festival of the Passover. The Fathers of the Christian church were perturbed by its erotic charge, its voluptuous incitation. They assumed that a sacred text must have a spiritual meaning. As Origen wrote in the third century, 'If these things are not to be understood spiritually, are they not simply fabulous tales? If they have no hidden mystery, are they not unworthy of God?' The *Song* became part of an intricate web of allegorical readings of Scripture. These readings constructed both the theology and the poetry of a religion centred on the historical incarnation of the eternal and spiritual. The *Song* became also an extraordinary paradox – a rich, fleshy metaphor for the divine longing that would cause the wise soul to reject the flesh and its desires. Origen's explication turned on the doubleness of the Latin word, *amor*, love, which was used to describe carnal desire and spiritual yearning. Origen himself went as far as self-castration in his search for pure spiritual love. He allegorised the Bride's withdrawal into the marriage chamber as the withdrawal of the pure soul from all extraneous earthly desires.

Origen identified the Bride with Ecclesia, the embattled,

---

* The queen said, 'Seven there are and nine that enter, two yield the draught and one drinks.' Said he to her: 'Seven are the days of a woman's defilement, and nine the months of pregnancy, two are the breasts that yield the draught and one the child that drinks it.' Whereupon she said to him, 'Thou art wise.' Louis Ginzberg, *Legends of the Bible*, pp. 560 ff.

sinful Christian church, who had to learn to respond to the loving care and demands of her Divine Spouse, Christ. The *Song*'s imagery of the bridegroom knocking at a locked door, the bride waking too late, became assimilated to Christ's own parable of the sleepy, unwatchful bridesmaidens. In the twelfth century commentators interpreted the *Song* in terms of the Virgin Mary, the Mother-Bride, the sister-spouse, the mediator. The allegory had for them a literal historical meaning, to be teased out. The Bride also became the Hetaira, romantic heroine and childlike maiden, wooed by Christ the very perfect knight. Poems about Mary Magdalene, repentant beauty, spiritual sinner, who broke an alabaster vase of precious ointment over her Lord's feet, used the imagery of the *Song*. The spiritual interpreters, most strikingly St Bernard of Clairvaux, in his sermons on *The Song of Songs*, saw the individual human soul itself as the Beloved, drawn towards Christ initially through love of the created world. The Latin word for the soul is *anima*, which is a feminine word, and it is striking that the allegorical commentaries and interpretations of the *Song* written by celibate monks, take the passive, open, receptive female consciousness as the central consciousness of the drama. The human soul, male or female, in this erotic mysticism, is a woman waiting for her master, her lord, her bridegroom. The saint's rhetoric, like his vision of the *Song*, includes the erotic, lingers over it, only to dismiss it.

> You must not give an earth-bound meaning to this colouring of corruptible flesh, to this red liquid suffused beneath her pearly skin, to enhance her bodily beauty

in the pink and white loveliness of her cheeks. For the substance of the soul is incorporeal and invisible …

Or

Shall we imagine for ourselves a huge powerful man, gripped by love for an absent girl, rushing to her desired embraces, bounding over those mountains and hills which we see raised up so high over the plain that their summit seems to penetrate the clouds? It is certainly not proper to fabricate bodily fantasies in this way, and especially when treating of this spiritual Song … *

And St Bernard, preaching to the abbots of his order, on 'remembering the breasts' makes them into imagined women and mothers: 'Be gentle, avoid harshness, give up blows, show your breasts: let your bosoms be fat with milk, not swollen with wrath.'

The fathers of the church were preaching an incarnate God to an incarnate congregation, creatures made up of flesh and spirit. They could rationalise their treatment of *The Song of Songs* – which is not a rational structure – by saying that its inspired author had used the language of the flesh to entice the incarnate souls to the love of the Incarnate Word, speaking through the flesh. Their ingenuity and resourceful reconstructions and deconstructions can seem both beautiful

---

* These passages are quoted, with some retranslation, from Anne W Astell, *The Song of Songs in the Middle Ages* (Cornell University Press, 1990). I am much indebted to this excellent book.

and absurd to an unbeliever seduced and baffled by the literal presence of the *Song* itself. Is it the nature of the text or the nature of the theology that brings about all the building of these airy places, such a reader may ask her or himself.

The Jungians, as we might expect, have an answer. They are drawn to the *Song* by the presence of the woman and the idea of a marriage. The female persona in the story, or stories, can be seen as the Jungian *anima*, the complementary female self who must be integrated into the psyche for wholeness. The four major feminine archetypes of Jungian psychoanalysis – Virgin, Mother, Medial Woman and Hetaira – can all be found easily in the *Song*. A Jungian reading of the *Song* includes the alchemical Coniunctio, the mystical marriage of opposites. In alchemical terms the Shulamite's blackness signifies the 'feminine personification of the prima materia in the *nigredo* stato'. Jung quotes alchemical texts in which the Shulamite attributes her blackness to the original sin of Eve: 'O that the serpent roused up Eve! To which I must testify with the black colour that clings to me.' * 'She is the *anima mundi* or Gnostic Sophia, caught in the dark embraces of *physis*.' Here is a psychoanalytical and alchemical version of the interpretative anxiety about incarnation, spirit and matter. It leads to a consideration of the extraordinary proliferation of quotations, objects, metaphors from the *Song* throughout many centuries and literatures.

Ann Astell gives some beautiful examples of love lyrics, sacred and profane, from the Middle Ages. I myself found

---

* Jung, *Mysterium Coniunctionis*, Collected Works 14, para 591.

The Song of Songs everywhere in the thesis I never finished, which was about sensuous metaphors for the spiritual in the seventeenth century, and turned out to be about narratives of fleshly temptations in gardens, from Spenser's 'Bower of Bliss' to *Paradise Lost* and the temptation of Christ in *Paradise Regained*. The words of the *Song* sing enchantingly in English, for instance in Henry Vaughan's 'The Night'.

> God's silent searching flight
> When my Lord's head is filled with dew and all
> His locks are wet with the clear drops of night
> His still, soft call;
> His knocking time; the soul's dumb watch,
> When spirits her fair kinred catch.

Marvell's delightful conceits in 'The Nymph Complaining for the Death of her Fawn' combine classical pastoral with the *Song*'s imagery of innocence in a closed garden, lilies and roses, the beloved as a hart or a roe deer on the mountains. And Milton compares his Paradise garden to

> Those gardens feigned
> Or of revived Adonis, or renowned
> Alcinous, host of old Laertes' son,
> Or that, not mystic, where the sapient king
> Held dalliance with his fair Egyptian spouse.
> (*Paradise Lost*, IX, ll. 439-43)

Alastair Fowler, a great editor, points out that Milton is here drawing an analogy between Solomon and Adam, both wise, both uxorious, both lovers in gardens. He points out

introduction

the ambiguity of the word 'sapient', meaning, in its Latin root, 'gaining knowledge by tasting'. This concept, like most commentary on the Song, finds the spirit in the flesh. Fowler goes on to point out that Milton's references to 'sapience' in *The Song of Songs* tend to associate Solomon with Satan, and with the latter's interest in Eve's beauty, and in the taste of the apples of the Tree of the knowledge of Good and Evil. In *Paradise Lost* (Book v, ll. 40–8), Eve recounts to Adam a dream in which Satan tempts her in a parody of the lover of the *Song*. It is interesting in this context that Solomon turned to the worship of Ashtaroth through the persuasion of his wives.

> For it came to pass, when Solomon was old, that his wives turned away his heart after other gods: and his heart was not perfect with the Lord his God, as was the heart of David his father.
>
> For Solomon went after Ashtoreth the goddess of the Zidonians, and after Milcom, the abomination of the Ammonites … (*1 Kings* 11 : 4-5)

St Augustine, before Milton, compared the sins of Adam and Solomon, led into temptation by their love for their wives. Modern scholars see *The Song of Songs* as an echo of something more ancient, the marriage songs of the sacred marriages of the ancient Mesopotamian gods and goddesses, Inana and Dumuzi, Ishtar and Tammuz, gods whose worship entailed sacred prostitution, the making of gardens, the mourning of the vanished young god and the celebration of his return with the spring. These deities were, in some versions, brother and sister – 'my sister, my spouse'. The return

and the rebirth of Adonis (who was the same god as Tam-
muz, since Adonis simply means 'Lord') coincided with the
Spring, and the return of vegetation.

> For, lo, the winter is past, the rain is over and gone;
> The flowers appear on the earth;
> the time of the singing of birds is come,
> and the voice of the turtle is heard in our land;
> The fig tree putteth forth her green figs,
> and the vines with the tender grape
> give a good smell. Arise, my love, my fair one,
> and come away.

Frazer, in *The Golden Bough*, compares the kings of the
Bible to the priest-kings of the Syrian Lord Adonis, and
quotes St Jerome, who 'tells us that Bethlehem, the tradi-
tional birthplace of the Lord, was shaded by a grove of that
still older Syrian Lord Adonis, and that where the infant Jesus
had wept, the lover of Venus was bewailed.' Jerome, Frazer
says, appears to have believed that the grove was planted by
heathens to defile the sacred spot. Frazer himself believes
that the grove was older, and that in any case the Christian
god who was the bread of life, born in Bethlehem, 'the House
of Bread' was related to the older corn spirit.

Whatever the spiritual meanings and antecedents, the
immediate experience of reading the *Song* is both sensuously
exciting and baffling. As a narrative, it does not hold together.
Moments of intense dramatic feeling – the Shulamite's
description of her rejected blackness, the knocking and
vanishing of the bridegroom, her wandering the streets of

Jerusalem, the unidentified 'we' expressing concern for their little sister who has no breasts – all these are both entirely memorable and fleeting. The same, in a different way, can be said of the descriptions, concrete and metaphorical, of the bodies of the lovers. The woman is seen as a city with walls and turrets, as a garden enclosed and a fountain sealed, as an army with banners, as a flock of goats, as sheep, as corn and wine, as perfumes. She is both vividly solid and somehow diffused into city, army, riches and jewels, the landscape of pastoral herdsmen, and orchards with every kind of tree. I remember my first bewildered reading, as a western child with a compulsory Bible in her desk, of this dreamworld. What corresponded to that longing for love with which we are all born (or so I supposed) were powerful abstract phrases: 'For love is as strong as death; jealousy is cruel as the grave: the coals thereof are coals of fire, which hath a most vehement flame.'

There was something deliciously disturbing about all the liquids, the milk, wine and honey, something tantalising about the glimpses of bodies and doors. But many of the specific metaphors were disturbing differently – 'thy teeth are as a flock of sheep which go up from the washing, whereof every one beareth twins, and there is not one barren among them.' The analogy between teeth and sheep (whiteness, similarity) seems tenuous, and is made more tenuous by the overloading of the twins and the fertility – it is as though, I intuited even as a child, the speaker is a shepherd congratulating himself on the abundance of his possessions, flocks and women. There is something immediately powerful, in most cultures,

I should think, about the virginal images: 'A garden enclosed is my sister, my spouse, a spring shut up, a fountain sealed.'

The image of woman as tree – 'this thy stature is like to a palm tree and thy breasts like clusters of grapes' – allows the imagination to make and combine both flesh and plant. But again and again this is simply not possible. There is an element of excess, of too much, too much fruit, too many riches, too much landscape, too much architecture, eyes like fish-pools, nose like a tower of Lebanon, breasts like twin roes, a creature who in one verse is fair as the moon, clear as the sun, and terrible as an army with banners. When the navel is compared to a round goblet, which wanteth not liquor and the belly is immediately afterwards compared to a heap of wheat set about with lilies, the effect is to make the wine and wheat richly present and the human body shadowy, vanishing, mysterious. Everything is present, the lovers are a whole world, rich and strange, metamorphosed by the poetic, or religious imagination, into both the natural world and the world of human artefacts and precious things. The winds blow from both north and south, the sun and the moon both shine, fountains, wells and streams are full of living water. And the more the metaphors are heaped up, the more they become interchangeable, the more the desire which sings in the *Song* becomes a polymorphous celebration of everything.

Or perhaps of itself, which is why I have always preferred to call it *The Song of Songs*, rather than *The Song of Solomon*. It is a poem about the making of poetry, the naming of the world, the construction of the world by the human imagination, powered by the erotic desire which both Freud and

Darwin celebrated also. Later English poets learned from it a kind of eastern poetry which was diffused and exceeding, rather than precise and contained. The mythical erotic English gardens of Tennyson's *Maud* owe much to the *Song*. Tennyson combines his Isle of Wight cedars with the cedars of Lebanon, as he combines the lilies and roses of the *Song* with an English garden. Browning complained that Tennyson had diffused the feeling that should have been applied to the woman into the landscape. But Tennyson knew what he was doing. He had been reading Persian poetry, and understanding the *Song* in his way.

The *Song* continues to haunt our imaginations, between the absurd and the sublime. Dorothy Sayers' *Busman's Honeymoon* quotes it absurdly. Harriet Vane, watching Lord Peter Wimsey in a blazer, reflects that she has 'married England'. But her lord, on waking after their wedding night, addresses her as 'my Shulamite'.

And in quite another world, the *Song* inhabits some of the greatest and most terrible poetry of our time, the poems in German of Paul Celan. The figure of Shulamith, whose name occurs only once in the Bible, appears in many forms in his work. His riddling poems about terror and loss, about the Holocaust and Israel, mourn both the Rose of Sharon, and, specifically, 'my sister, my spouse', the lost and destroyed. His biographer, John Felstiner, traces the tradition by which Shulamith, whose name is associated with *Shalom* * (peace),

---

* Edward F. Edinger, *The Bible and the Psyche* (Inner City Books, 1986) p. 137.

was seen by the mystical tradition as a figure both for the
Shechinah (the divine light) and for the promised return to
Zion. 'Return, return, O Shulamite; return, return, that we
may look upon thee.' * She appears in *Todesfuge* (*Deathfugue*)
in a repeated, chanted juxtaposition with the doomed Mar-
garet of Goethe's *Faust*.

> Dein goldenes Haar Margarete
> Dein aschenes Haar Sulamith

> (your golden hair, Margareta,
> your ashen hair, Shulamith)

Here, Shulamith's burned blackness, her ashen hair, are
irredeemable, made smoke, buried in the air. Her darkness
cancels and darkens Margarete's innocent suffering. This new,
dreadful figuration of Shulamith ends a poem as powerful
and unforgettable as the *Song* itself. It adds a meaning and a
figure that can never again be separated from the changing
poetic world of the *Song*, whatever else may be added.

* John Felstiner, *Paul Celan, Poet, Survivor, Jew* (Yale, 1995).

the song of solomon

The song of songs, which is Solomon's.

  ² Let him kiss me with the kisses of his mouth;
   for thy love is better than wine.
  ³ Because of the savour of thy good ointments
   thy name is as ointment poured forth,
    therefore do the virgins love thee.
  ⁴ Draw me, we will run after thee;
   the king hath brought me into his chambers:
    we will be glad and rejoice in thee,
   we will remember thy love more than wine:
    the upright love thee.
  ⁵ I am black, but comely,
   O ye daughters of Jerusalem,
    as the tents of Kedar,
   as the curtains of Solomon.
  ⁶ Look not upon me, because I am black,
   because the sun hath looked upon me.
    My mother's children were angry with me;
   they made me the keeper of the vineyards;
    but mine own vineyard have I not kept.
  ⁷ Tell me, O thou whom my soul loveth,
   where thou feedest,

where thou makest thy flock to rest at noon;
for why should I be as one that turneth aside
by the flocks of thy companions?

⁸ If thou know not, O thou fairest among women,
go thy way forth by the footsteps of the flock,
and feed thy kids beside the shepherds' tents.

⁹ I have compared thee, O my love,
to a company of horses in Pharaoh's chariots.

¹⁰ Thy cheeks are comely with rows of jewels,
thy neck with chains of gold.

¹¹ We will make thee borders of gold
with studs of silver.

¹² While the king sitteth at his table,
my spikenard sendeth forth the smell thereof.

¹³ A bundle of myrrh is my wellbeloved unto me;
he shall lie all night betwixt my breasts.

¹⁴ My beloved is unto me as a cluster of camphire
in the vineyards of En-gedi.

¹⁵ Behold, thou art fair, my love;
behold, thou art fair; thou hast doves' eyes.

¹⁶ Behold, thou art fair, my beloved,
yea, pleasant:
also our bed is green.

¹⁷ The beams of our house are cedar,
and our rafters of fir.

2   I am the rose of Sharon,
and the lily of the valleys.

² As the lily among thorns,

so is my love among the daughters.
³As the apple tree among the trees of the wood,
so is my beloved among the sons.
I sat down under his shadow with great delight,
and his fruit was sweet to my taste.
⁴He brought me to the banqueting house,
and his banner over me was love.
⁵Stay me with flagons, comfort me with apples;
for I am sick of love.
⁶His left hand is under my head,
and his right hand doth embrace me.
⁷I charge you, O ye daughters of Jerusalem,
by the roes, and by the hinds of the field,
that ye stir not up,
nor awake my love, till he please.
⁸The voice of my beloved!
Behold, he cometh leaping upon the mountains,
skipping upon the hills.
⁹My beloved is like a roe or a young hart;
behold, he standeth behind our wall,
he looketh forth at the windows,
shewing himself through the lattice.
¹⁰My beloved spake, and said unto me,
'Rise up, my love, my fair one, and come away.
¹¹For, lo, the winter is past,
the rain is over and gone;
¹²the flowers appear on the earth;
the time of the singing of birds is come,
and the voice of the turtle is heard in our land;

¹³ the fig tree putteth forth her green figs,
　　and the vines with the tender grape
　　　　give a good smell.
　　Arise, my love, my fair one, and come away.
¹⁴ O my dove, that art in the clefts of the rock,
　　in the secret places of the stairs,
　　　　let me see thy countenance,
　　let me hear thy voice;
　　　　for sweet is thy voice,
　　and thy countenance is comely.
¹⁵ Take us the foxes,
　　the little foxes, that spoil the vines;
　　　　for our vines have tender grapes.'
¹⁶ My beloved is mine, and I am his;
　　he feedeth among the lilies.
¹⁷ Until the day break,
　　and the shadows flee away,
　　　　turn, my beloved, and be thou like a roe
　　or a young hart upon the mountains of Bether.

3 By night on my bed I sought him
　　whom my soul loveth;
　　　　I sought him, but I found him not.
² I will rise now, and go about the city in the streets,
　　and in the broad ways I will seek
　　　　him whom my soul loveth:
　　I sought him, but I found him not.
³ The watchmen that go about the city found me:
　　to whom I said,

'Saw ye him whom my soul loveth?'
⁴ It was but a little that I passed from them,
　　but I found him whom my soul loveth:
　　　　I held him, and would not let him go,
　　until I had brought him into my mother's house,
　　　　and into the chamber of her that conceived me.
⁵ I charge you, O ye daughters of Jerusalem,
　　by the roes, and by the hinds of the field,
　　　　that ye stir not up,
　　nor awake my love, till he please.
⁶ Who is this that cometh out of the wilderness
　　like pillars of smoke,
　　　　perfumed with myrrh and frankincense,
　　with all powders of the merchant?
⁷ Behold his bed, which is Solomon's;
　　threescore valiant men are about it,
　　　　of the valiant of Israel.
⁸ They all hold swords, being expert in war;
　　every man hath his sword upon his thigh
　　　　because of fear in the night.
⁹ King Solomon made himself a chariot of
　　the wood of Lebanon.
¹⁰ He made the pillars thereof of silver,
　　the bottom thereof of gold,
　　　　the covering of it of purple,
　　the midst thereof being paved with love,
　　　　for the daughters of Jerusalem.
¹¹ Go forth, O ye daughters of Zion,
　　and behold king Solomon with the crown

wherewith his mother crowned him
in the day of his espousals,
and in the day of the gladness of his heart.

4 Behold, thou art fair, my love;
behold, thou art fair;
thou hast doves' eyes within thy locks;
thy hair is as a flock of goats,
that appear from mount Gilead.
2 Thy teeth are like a flock of sheep that are even shorn,
which came up from the washing;
whereof every one bear twins,
and none is barren among them.
3 Thy lips are like a thread of scarlet,
and thy speech is comely:
thy temples are like a piece of
a pomegranate within thy locks.
4 Thy neck is like the tower of David
builded for an armoury,
whereon there hang a thousand bucklers,
all shields of mighty men.
5 Thy two breasts are like two young roes
that are twins, which feed among the lilies.
6 Until the day break, and the shadows flee away,
I will get me to the mountain of myrrh,
and to the hill of frankincense.
7 Thou art all fair, my love; there is no spot in thee.
8 Come with me from Lebanon, my spouse,
with me from Lebanon;

look from the top of Amana,
from the top of Shenir and Hermon,
from the lions' dens,
from the mountains of the leopards.
⁹ Thou hast ravished my heart, my sister, my spouse;
thou hast ravished my heart with
one of thine eyes, with one chain of thy neck.
¹⁰ How fair is thy love, my sister, my spouse!
How much better is thy love than wine!
And the smell of thine ointments than all spices!
¹¹ Thy lips, O my spouse, drop as the honeycomb:
honey and milk are under thy tongue;
and the smell of thy garments
is like the smell of Lebanon.
¹² A garden inclosed is my sister, my spouse;
a spring shut up, a fountain sealed.
¹³ Thy plants are an orchard of pomegranates,
with pleasant fruits;
camphire, with spikenard,
¹⁴ spikenard and saffron;
calamus and cinnamon,
with all trees of frankincense;
myrrh and aloes,
with all the chief spices:
¹⁵ a fountain of gardens,
a well of living waters,
and streams from Lebanon.
¹⁶ Awake, O north wind; and come, thou south;
blow upon my garden,

that the spices thereof may flow out.
Let my beloved come into his garden,
and eat his pleasant fruits.

5 I am come into my garden, my sister, my spouse:
I have gathered my myrrh with my spice;
I have eaten my honeycomb with my honey;
I have drunk my wine with my milk:
eat, O friends; drink,
yea, drink abundantly, O beloved.
[2] I sleep, but my heart waketh:
it is the voice of my beloved that knocketh, saying,
'Open to me, my sister, my love,
my dove, my undefiled;
for my head is filled with dew,
and my locks with the drops of the night.'
[3] I have put off my coat; how shall I put it on?
I have washed my feet; how shall I defile them?
[4] My beloved put in his hand by the hole of the door,
and my bowels were moved for him.
[5] I rose up to open to my beloved;
and my hands dropped with myrrh,
and my fingers with sweet-smelling myrrh,
upon the handles of the lock.
[6] I opened to my beloved;
but my beloved had withdrawn himself,
and was gone:
my soul failed when he spake:
I sought him, but I could not find him;

I called him, but he gave me no answer.
⁷ The watchmen that went about the city found me,
    they smote me, they wounded me;
        the keepers of the walls
    took away my veil from me.
⁸ I charge you, O daughters of Jerusalem,
    if ye find my beloved, that ye tell him,
        that I am sick of love.
⁹ What is thy beloved more than another beloved,
    O thou fairest among women?
        What is thy beloved more than another beloved,
    that thou dost so charge us?
¹⁰ My beloved is white and ruddy,
    the chiefest among ten thousand.
¹¹ His head is as the most fine gold,
    his locks are bushy, and black as a raven.
¹² His eyes are as the eyes of doves
    by the rivers of waters,
        washed with milk, and fitly set.
¹³ His cheeks are as a bed of spices,
    as sweet flowers:
        his lips like lilies,
    dropping sweet smelling myrrh.
¹⁴ His hands are as gold rings set with the beryl:
    his belly is as bright ivory
        overlaid with sapphires.
¹⁵ His legs are as pillars of marble,
    set upon sockets of fine gold;
        his countenance is as Lebanon,

excellent as the cedars.
¹⁶ His mouth is most sweet;
yea, he is altogether lovely.
This is my beloved, and this is my friend,
O daughters of Jerusalem.

6 Whither is thy beloved gone,
O thou fairest among women?
Whither is thy beloved turned aside?
That we may seek him with thee.
² My beloved is gone down into his garden,
to the beds of spices,
to feed in the gardens, and to gather lilies.
³ I am my beloved's, and my beloved is mine;
he feedeth among the lilies.
⁴ Thou art beautiful, O my love, as Tirzah,
comely as Jerusalem,
terrible as an army with banners.
⁵ Turn away thine eyes from me,
for they have overcome me:
thy hair is as a flock of goats
that appear from Gilead.
⁶ Thy teeth are as a flock of sheep
which go up from the washing,
whereof every one beareth twins,
and there is not one barren among them.
⁷ As a piece of a pomegranate
are thy temples within thy locks.
⁸ There are threescore queens,

and fourscore concubines,
and virgins without number.

⁹ My dove, my undefiled is but one;
she is the only one of her mother,
she is the choice one of her that bare her.
The daughters saw her, and blessed her;
yea, the queens and the concubines,
and they praised her.

¹⁰ Who is she that looketh forth as the morning,
fair as the moon, clear as the sun,
and terrible as an army with banners?

¹¹ I went down into the garden of nuts
to see the fruits of the valley,
and to see whether the vine flourished,
and the pomegranates budded.

¹² Or ever I was aware,
my soul made me like the chariots of Ammi-nadib.

¹³ Return, return, O Shulamite;
return, return, that we may look upon thee.
What will ye see in the Shulamite?
As it were the company of two armies.

7 How beautiful are thy feet with shoes,
O prince's daughter!
The joints of thy thighs are like jewels,
the work of the hands of a cunning workman.

² Thy navel is like a round goblet,
which wanteth not liquor;
thy belly is like an heap of wheat

set about with lilies.
³ Thy two breasts are like two young roes that are twins.
⁴ Thy neck is as a tower of ivory;
thine eyes like the fishpools in Heshbon,
by the gate of Bath-rabbim;
thy nose is as the tower of Lebanon
which looketh toward Damascus.
⁵ Thine head upon thee is like Carmel,
and the hair of thine head like purple;
the king is held in the galleries.
⁶ How fair and how pleasant art thou,
O love, for delights!
⁷ This thy stature is like to a palm tree,
and thy breasts to clusters of grapes.
⁸ I said, 'I will go up to the palm tree,
I will take hold of the boughs thereof:
now also thy breasts shall be
as clusters of the vine,
and the smell of thy nose like apples;
⁹ and the roof of thy mouth like the best wine
for my beloved, that goeth down sweetly,
causing the lips of those that are asleep
to speak.'
¹⁰ I am my beloved's, and his desire is toward me.
¹¹ Come, my beloved,
let us go forth into the field;
let us lodge in the villages.
¹² Let us get up early to the vineyards;
let us see if the vine flourish,

whether the tender grape appear,
and the pomegranates bud forth;
there will I give thee my loves.
¹³ The mandrakes give a smell,
and at our gates are all manner of pleasant fruits,
new and old, which I have laid up for thee,
O my beloved.

8

O that thou wert as my brother,
that sucked the breasts of my mother!
When I should find thee without,
I would kiss thee;
yea, I should not be despised.
² I would lead thee,
and bring thee into my mother's house,
who would instruct me;
I would cause thee to drink of spiced wine
of the juice of my pomegranate.
³ His left hand should be under my head,
and his right hand should embrace me.
⁴ I charge you, O daughters of Jerusalem,
that ye stir not up,
nor awake my love, until he please.
⁵ Who is this that cometh up from the wilderness,
leaning upon her beloved?
I raised thee up under the apple tree:
there thy mother brought thee forth;
there she brought thee forth that bare thee.
⁶ Set me as a seal upon thine heart,

as a seal upon thine arm;
for love is strong as death;
jealousy is cruel as the grave;
the coals thereof are coals of fire,
which hath a most vehement flame.
[7] Many waters cannot quench love,
neither can the floods drown it;
if a man would give
all the substance of his house for love,
it would utterly be contemned.
[8] We have a little sister, and she hath no breasts;
what shall we do for our sister
in the day when she shall be spoken for?
[9] If she be a wall,
we will build upon her a palace of silver;
and if she be a door,
we will inclose her with boards of cedar.
[10] I am a wall, and my breasts like towers;
then was I in his eyes as one that found favour.
[11] Solomon had a vineyard at Baalhamon;
he let out the vineyard unto keepers;
every one for the fruit thereof
was to bring a thousand pieces of silver.
[12] My vineyard, which is mine, is before me;
thou, O Solomon, must have a thousand,
and those that keep the fruit thereof
two hundred.
[13] Thou that dwellest in the gardens,
the companions hearken to thy voice;

cause me to hear it.
14 Make haste, my beloved,
and be thou like to a roe or to a young hart
upon the mountains of spices.

titles in the series

genesis – *introduced by steven rose*
exodus – *introduced by david grossman*
job – *introduced by louis de bernières*
proverbs – *introduced by charles johnson*
ecclesiastes – *introduced by doris lessing*
song of solomon – *introduced by a s byatt*
matthew – *introduced by a n wilson*
mark – *introduced by nick cave*
luke – *introduced by richard holloway*
john – *introduced by blake morrison*
corinthians – *introduced by fay weldon*
revelation – *introduced by will self*